www.uuclassconversations.org

Follow us on Facebook
https://www.facebook.com/uuclassconversations

Publication Date: December 2022
Copyright - UU Class Conversations
BISAC: REL103000
RELIGION / Unitarian Universalism

IBSN: 978-1-38-783091-6

9 781387 830916

Meditations on Class is dedicated to those
who are working to
dismantle classism within our congregations
and communities and to
those who so willing gave us the
gift of their work to share with you.
We are eternally grateful.
Thank you!

Meditations on Class

Sidewalks

I didn't used to think about sidewalks much. Not even in college or immediately after, when we walked everywhere because we didn't have a vehicle. I went to college in a compact, eminently walkable small town, but even so, I believe I logged 4 plus miles every day. Looking back on it, I can't believe I walked that much. Like I said, I didn't think about sidewalks. I just walked on them. Sometimes I climbed over the snow banks, sometimes I slid on the ice, sometimes I slogged through the mud of the off-sidewalk shortcut, but I didn't really think about the sidewalks.

When I moved to a bigger town, I had a more difficult time walking because the town's neighborhoods are not easily connected to the downtown area and are not very walkable. This appears intentional. According to the city ordinances, all new neighborhoods after 1998 must not have straight thoroughfares directly across them and must have winding roads (older neighborhoods were grandfathered in).

After my baby was born, I discovered that the places I just strolled over by myself were major obstacles with a stroller. Canals with no sidewalk along them or major intersections with only stop signs became places that frightened me. How could I run across a 4-way stop intersection with 2 lanes in each direction with a stroller? Although I no longer needed to walk (we now had a reliable vehicle), walking was the only form of transportation for many who did not have access to personal transportation. These sidewalks were vital arteries to the community and to needed resources.

When my baby was almost a year old, we moved into a house in one of the older neighborhoods in our town. It was easier to walk with the stroller—blocks and blocks of quiet neighborhood streets without busy intersections. But here I discovered another problem: the sidewalks were in pretty bad shape with large cracks, shifted sections where one section was several inches higher than the neighboring one, holes, and even non-existent sections. I became an expert at lifting the stroller up and over the many obstructions we encountered on our walks.

The more I walked, the more I noticed another problem. I didn't just have to lift the stroller over frost heaves and root uprisings, I often had to lift it over the curbs at the intersections. There were no curb cuts at many of the intersections (a curb cut is the place where the curb dips down to meet the gutter at a driveway, intersection, or parking area). A proper curb cut usually has a yellow pad with raised dimples to alert blind walkers using a cane that they are approaching an intersection.

About this same time, I began writing opinion pieces for the local newspaper. I decided to write one of my first columns on the sidewalks in the town and their terrible condition.

After the column was published, I got a surprise. Individuals in wheelchairs called and wrote to tell me how much they appreciated my column and how badly they needed better sidewalks. For people with different mobility, sidewalks can grant or block access to buildings for both recreation and much-needed resources.

I wrote a couple more columns on sidewalks, attracting more attention each time. After those columns, the city applied for and received a federal grant to improve sidewalk conditions in the business districts of town by adding curb cuts and yellow pads.

My town also has a city government program where the city will pay for homeowners to fix their sidewalks if they cannot afford to do so themselves. When I suggested this program to my neighbor, she told me she couldn't use the program. Why? Because the program was a reimbursement program. She would have to pay up-front to have the sidewalks fixed and then be reimbursed by the city. She did not have the up-front money, and there were no alternatives in the city program.

When I watch the people going past my window, I see my neighbors walking their dogs, I see children going back and forth to school, I sometimes see mothers with strollers, I see white men riding bicycles in the street to work – they are usually dressed in professional attire, and I see Latinos and Latinas walking with groceries and backpacks – going to and from the store and work.

Or, to put it another way, I see a variety of people from different class groups and ethnic backgrounds using the sidewalks. For some of them, riding bikes and walking are choices that make them, their children, pets, and the planet healthier. For others, these are the only forms of transportation they can afford. If I lived near the business districts, I would also see people in wheelchairs or with canes relying on the sidewalks to enter and exit buildings.

Sidewalks are an important shared part of a community's life. They are not a luxury item that can be neglected. The health of our sidewalks directly affects the safety of the people who rely on them every day. Sidewalks are a class issue and a disability issue.

Elizabeth Cogliati

Kansas, 1937

I'd ride astride Old Major
holding tight to the harness
when Daddy said "giddyup "
and that old plow horse pulled
and plodded slow up and down the field
when Gee or Haw was called
Major would dance until he faced the way we'd come
I'd twist to see my Dad
sweat dripping from his chin,
his shirt stained sky blue
swing wide around to turn
plow lines tied over one shoulder and under the other
all his strength and weight
harnessed to the handles of the plow
as we gouged deep gashes in the earth
like brown corduroy.

Barbara Cogswell

White Woman's Burden

push Down Button
wait – door opens
note wing tip shoes
enclosed space
feel fear
note male in far corner - black
feel shame of fear
palpable moment
before entering
rueful smile to self
man looks down
I leave space first
awkwardness dissipates
past experiences recalled
drive home
months later
write poem

Barbara Cogswell

Coming Home: Engaging the Wealthy to Reverse Inequality

The extreme levels of inequality in our society are painful to behold. As someone who was "born on third base," I watch these polarizations and know that no good will come of them. Do we - including the 1 percent - really want to live in an economic apartheid society? All the evidence now suggests that too much inequality is bad for everyone, even the super-rich.

There are many reasons why we need to rethink our predicament, but for a moment let's consider this one, which in many ways trumps them all: As a planet, we are experiencing an ecological crisis that will transform our daily lives. Climate change and ocean acidification - along with breaches of other planetary boundaries - will alter our food and energy systems and transform our way of life.

There have been recent news accounts about billionaires buying mountain fortresses in the Rockies and "get away" farms in New Zealand with airplane landing strips. These escape fantasies are delusional thinking. The island paradises will be swamped from rising sea level. The mountain redoubts will be choked with the smoke of burning forests. It is in no one's interest to continue operating as if a few privileged people are going to escape on a spaceship or retreat to a mountaintop enclave.

The ecological catastrophe at our door will wipe out our most treasured asset - our natural ecosystems, which are the foundations of all private wealth. What is wealth without clean water and healthy oceans? What is wealth on a degraded earth? As scientist Johan Rockstrom writes, "We're still blind, despite all the science, to the fact that wealth in the world depends on the health of the planet."

All of humanity - billionaire hedge fund managers, suburban soccer moms and Bangladeshi farmers - is now bound together, our fate linked to our ability to respond to a planetary challenge bigger than anything we've faced before. At the same time, we are confronting a societal challenge of unprecedented inequality. The accelerating polarization of income, wealth and opportunity is moving us quickly to a society that no one will want to live in, including the most privileged.

As French economist Thomas Piketty has argued, if we don't intervene in the current economic system, wealth and power will continue to concentrate in fewer and fewer hands. We are moving toward a society governed by a hereditary aristocracy of wealth.

The wealthy have already hijacked our democracy. Roughly a year before the 2016 presidential election, nearly half the money in the campaign had come from just 158 families, many of them billionaires. Realities like this have led former president Jimmy Carter to describe our political system as an oligarchy.

Younger people and people of color especially are feeling the brunt of this polarization, with deteriorating livelihoods, crushing debt, and stagnant wages. All these forces undermine opportunity and quality of life for everyone.

The debate over solutions to growing inequality is polarized and stuck in the old story of class deservedness and antagonism. We must find a way to disrupt these antiquated narratives and propose a way forward.

My message to the planet's most wealthy and privileged citizens - my own people in the top 1 to 5 percent of the nation - is to "come home," to make a commitment to place, to put down a stake, and work for an economy that works for everyone. Coming home means sharing our wealth and paying our fair share of taxes. It means moving investment capital out of the old fossil-fuel economy, offshore accounts, and speculative financial investments - and redirecting it to the new relocalized economy, including regional food and energy systems and enterprises that broaden wealth ownership, such as cooperatives.

The privileged must stand with the 99 percent to defend our communities against the worst aspects of predatory capitalism, joining in solidarity against the rapacious rich. But to succeed, we need allies among the reachable wealthy. We must find ways to engage and invite the 1 percent home, back to the table, to be partners in transforming the future.

Where there are opportunities to win allies, I urge us all to proceed with empathy, adopting powerful tactics of active love and nonviolent direct action to make this happen. Instead of a class war of shame, I advocate an appeal to common humanity and empathy. This shift in tactics will help open new possibilities.

There is good news. A movement of what I call "open-hearted wealthy people" understands that their genuine self-interest is inextricably linked to the rest of humanity and our ability to fix the future. They want to "come home," reestablish a stake in the commonweal, and commit their time, networks, skills, and capital to building healthy, equitable, and resilient communities.

There is a new economy emerging in the shell of the old economy. This includes people and enterprises rejecting the system of extractive and looting-based capitalism and embracing a "generative" economy that operates within the boundaries of nature and promotes equality, rather than division.

Our current modes of thinking about wealth, class and racial differences are preventing the transformation required of us. We need to rewire ourselves as a species and change the economic system that is destroying nature and producing escalating inequalities.[1]

Chuck Collins

---

[1] *See appendix for additional prompts and quotes suggested by Chuck Collins*

I Asked My Husband

"Why do you buy so many things?"
I asked my husband,
And my tone was not friendly.

"Whenever you think we're out of something—
Paper towels, nails, aluminum foil—
You rush to the store.
You don't even look
To see what we have."

My voice was filled with the confidence
Of certainty.
Of rightness.
Of how things are done.

He looked at me for a long time
And then said,
"Where you come from
Cabinets are full;
Things are bought in bulk,
There is always more for the having.
Where I come from
A dollar buys you
A split second dream of a future
Where cabinets are full
And things are bought in bulk
And there is always more for the having."

I sat and thought for a moment.
This was new to me.
"A dollar is meant to be spent,"
I said finally.
"Spent while you have it."
He nodded.
"Spent while you have it," he said.
"Spent on a dream."

"But you have so many dollars now," I said.

He thought for a long time
And as I watched his face
I saw his mother there
The one who had worked so long and so hard
For so little.
The one who so often told the heroic story of her parents
Walking from Mexico on wooden roads
But never spoke of heroism when she spoke of how she
Managed shopping malls and apartment buildings.

Maybe because being paid less than white men
To do the same job
Does not feel like heroism.

"Old habits die hard,"
My husband finally said.
He smiled sadly

And I knew he forgave me for not understanding before
And I hoped next time he wanted to buy something
He would be free from the judgment of my white gaze:
Paper towels, nails, aluminum foil, whatever
Bought in memory of ancestors who walked wooden roads
And mothers who suffered the sting of injustice.
And together he and I walked in the twilight
And considered tomorrow.

Jason Cook

You Say

You say everyone is welcome.
I'm glad to hear it.
You see, I know a young man without shoes.
He has sandals but no shoes right now.
He will someday; he is saving up.
He doesn't want the shoes from the shelter
Or any of the other giveaway places.
Those are for other people, he says.
People without homes.
People without jobs.
But he has a home
And he has a job.
He just doesn't have shoes
Not right now.
Besides, he wants good shoes
The kind he saw online.
The kind you buy just once
And take care of.
Not the kind he grew up with
Where the heel or the sole
Was always falling off.
Shoes that were new for just a few days
And then old and worn long past their time.
He wants good shoes
Good shoes for the first time.
Until then,
Is he welcome at your candlelit affair?
Is he welcome as part of your small talk
Of classical concerts and op-ed pieces
And environmentally friendly cars?
Are sandals appropriate for those conversations?
Or should he wait until he has shoes,
The right shoes?
The ones that fit your occasion?
Can you wait to hold your event
Until he does?
Or better yet,
Can you imagine a life
In which you don't have the right shoes?
Or any shoes at all?

Can you put on his shoes-
The ones he doesn't have-
And imagine that?

Jason Cook

We Are at Our Best in Community

Unitarian Universalism holds that the individual is the highest authority on their own spiritual health and well-being. No one can tell you what your relationship with the universe should be. We recognize that I cannot fully know and understand what your experiences are or how they have shaped you. But, we must be careful not to fall into the idolatry of the world around us, because the relationship is the thing that we strive for.

Covenantal Faith

Our faith is often called "covenantal." There is no statement of beliefs that you can recite privately to prove that you are a Unitarian Universalist. You have to make, and keep, a promise to a community.

You have to be a participant in relationships to be fully UU. You have to commit to allowing others to talk to you about your values and ideals and question their place in a responsible life.

You have to accept that you will be encouraged to grow your spirit, even when you are comfortable or growth seems hard. We believe that people are at their best when they are giving their best to the community.

It is easy to fall into the idolization of individuality. We all want to be the hero of our own story, and we want the credit for what we accomplish. But a story is no good without people to listen to it, and no one accomplishes anything in a vacuum. Your community, both in your church and beyond its walls, is at its best when we give everyone the opportunity to be an active participant and give their best back to the community.

Shared Responsibility

To do this, we need to be willing, as a community, to give some support and encouragement to people without them having to earn it on our terms. We need every child to receive a quality education, complete nutrition and adequate shelter. That is how we make them into responsible and compassionate citizens.

We need every person to be guaranteed free time from working to explore the things they love, whether that is painting, music, invention or math. This is how we foster invention and the creation of great art.

We need to address income inequality, as well as the classism behind it, so that those who are struggling can be more fully included in their community, having time and energy to participate. It builds a sense of belonging and shared responsibility.

We need to change how we view the social safety net – not as charity for those who are unable but as support for those who might be able to do more if encouraged and allowed.

We need to put community and a sense of shared responsibility on equal footing with individual achievement and success. Real success should factor in the benefits to the city, the nation and the world. People of every class need to be valued not just for what they have, but how they use their resources and how much they give back.

The United States is in danger of being poisoned by a toxic level of individualism. We've lost our civic-minded values, and our infrastructure and education are suffering because of it. We must rekindle the warmth of community if we are ever going to restore the fires of innovation and compassion.

Thomas Earthman

May I Live This Day

May I live this day
mindful of those in need of food at their table.

May I live this day
mindful of those in need of shelter for safety.

May I live this day
mindful of those in need of healthcare for their wellbeing.

May I live this day
mindful of those who need to earn not a minimum wage, but a living wage.

May I live this day
mindful of what I can do:
giving monetarily,
volunteering at shelters, food pantries, but more importantly
walking beside those in need .

May we live this day knowing we can do something,
knowing we are called to action, here and now
on this day and all the days that will follow.
Blessed Be and Amen.

Mike Greenwood

Is Fifteen Dollars a Living Wage?

Meet Sara. Not her real name.

Sara is not shy by any stretch of the imagination, actually she comes across as quite the extrovert — but she is too ashamed to show you her true face.

You probably have seen Sara. Perhaps you have passed her while driving in your car, or at the grocery story, at Dunkin Donuts, at the recreation fields or even here at CVUUS.

Sara is a mom who recently left her husband of 11 years. His mental health condition, fear of everything and everyone and increased use of drugs, intensified so much during this time of COVID that she became afraid of the severe negative impact it had on their two children ages 9 and 5 and the impact it would continue to have. So she decided to leave for their kids' mental wellness.

So where do you go when you leave you husband and you have 2 kids? Back home with mom and dad.

Sounds like a solid plan. Stay with mom and dad for a while, just until you get your feet back on the ground. Lots of others are doing this during COVID right? And it is only temporary.

Living at home with mom and dad was to be temporary of course. Just until she could get things figured out, get an apartment, and reestablish a life for herself and their children.

She had a reasonable income. After all she was making $14.95 an hour here in a public school, right here in our county, as a para educator. That $14.95 is real close, just a nickel off of what we all have come to know as the acceptable hourly wage for the working class. $15.00 an hour here in the land of Bernie Sanders. Our mantra is that $15.00 would be a living wage.

Affordable apartments are hard to find in our part of Vermont — and just about everywhere these days. But Sarah did find one after 3 months of searching. It was in a safe neighborhood, had a yard and was within walking distance to many amenities, including an elementary school.

17

It is a duplex apartment, 753 square feet. Not big but doable given her need to have her own place and get reestablished. Recently remodeled. Cost $1,500 a month.

Besides having a background and credit check, which is reasonable for a landlord to ask for, to rent this 753 square feet apartment you need to have 2 months' rent and another month's rent as security deposit. You can have a dog but that is an additional security deposit of $1,000.00.

For Sara that means she needed to have $4,500 just to sign the lease. And no dog.

So let's revisit our mantra of a living wage as $15.00 because I was there once believing it was a fair wage, not a great wage but a fair wage.

Two independent sources, Stratista and Massachusetts Institute of Technology, agree that a living wage in Addison County for a single adult and 2 children is $40.04 and that was in 2020. Sara makes less than half that amount. And for your information, in 2022, the federal minimum wage is still stagnant at $7.25 an hour and Vermont's minimum wage is $12.55.

When I sit with these numbers, $7.25 and $12.55 an hour, I have to ask myself, are these hourly wages a way we intentionally keep the poor poor? Is this our caste system?

Earning $15. 00 an hour, working 40 hours a week, an individual can't afford an apartment here in Addison County.

I share Sara's story with you as a reminder, first to myself and then for others, that there is a huge divide between the working class and the professional middle class. Somehow we think the $15 an hour is going to help a lot of people over that divide. It may help some, but I am afraid it is going to leave many behind. Sara included.

So what do we do? I do not have all the answers, I wish I did.

But first I need to applaud you, as this congregation has been steadfast in its exploration of class and classism. We even made changes in how we have raise money. My circle is not wide but I do interact with individuals from other UU congregations across the U.S. on a monthly basis and we are the only radical congregation that gives away free tickets to bid on items at an auction.

So what do we do? According to Bobbi Haro and her *Cycle of Liberation* the first thing we do is we self-educate and that is what we are doing today. I am going to suggest we share more of our class stories. I learn something about myself and others listening to them. So let's do that more often, share our stories as members of our church did today.

Bobbi's second step is to create community with people who are on board with us. Maybe we partner with an organization here in Addison County. Maybe we start our own organization. Maybe we invite those who are not making that $15.00 an hour to share their stories and let them tell us how we can help. Maybe work with Vermont Folklife Center and record stories to use in educating ourselves and others. The options are limitless.

Another of Bobbi's steps is we create change. We influence policy. We share and transform institutions. I am going to suggest we do another class audit here at CVUUS, we did one some 6 years ago. From worship to fundraising, are there classist elements that we can address in the style or way we do things here at CVUUS? Perhaps we let our elected representatives know about what we learned here today realizing that legislative change is not quick but slow. Oh my, is it slow. It has been more than 5 years talking about that$15.00 living wage. Maybe when talking with our neighbors and the conversation rolls around to schools as it usually does, we share Sara's story. We educate.

There are other pieces to Bobbi's Cycle of Liberation but this is a start if we engage in these three things - educate, build community and influence policy.

Let us begin to do just that.

Jackie Robinson said, "A life is not important except in the impact it has on other lives."

I would amend that to say, 'A life is not important except in the *positive* impact it has on other lives.'

Let us begin with making a positive impact by working for a truly living wage here within our own neighborhoods.

May it be so. Blessed be.

Mike Greenwood

A Simple Faith

Doug Muder, a contributing editor for <u>UU World,</u> in his article *Not My Father's Religion: Unitarian Universalism and the Working Class* (Fall 2007) doubted if our church could speak to the average working person. He thought that we didn't have anything to say to his father who made cattle feed in Illinois. If his father came to church he wouldn't find anyone he could talk with. He also said that you wouldn't find a trucker or anybody with callused hands. A harsh life needed a harsh religion. Being part of UU works for teachers and professors, but not for regular people. He thinks we exclude people by class. Doug Muder hopes we have a wider message, but he doesn't know what it is. To say the least, I was floored.

I hadn't noticed the article right away probably because it came out the year my father died. My father was a UU and a farmer. When he started working away from home he was a hired man. He cleaned barns, fed pigs, delivered calves and milked cows. He told about working for several weeks but was paid barely enough for gas to get home. Why my father joined our church is part of my answer to this article.

My father had grown up in within a Christian church, but then it came time for the dreaded confirmation class. He couldn't understand what he was supposed to agree to. He had no trouble with the Golden Rule and the Ten Commandments — except getting them in order. Telling the truth and keeping your hands off other people's things made sense. On the other hand, what about the Trinity and the dual nature of Christ? He didn't understand it. My Grandfather suggested he could wait until he grew up and then he would only have to say, "yes."

He got through this much of joining the church until his Uncle Jens died. I remember Uncle Jens. He never got farther than working at a feed store or for room and board somewhere. He liked ladies and children well enough. He probably would have liked to have his own family but where would he have ever earned enough money? So for the time, he was a bachelor Norwegian farmer. When he had a little extra he would buy my father and sisters ice cream or candy. Later, he did the same thing for me and even found a handkerchief to give me for my birthday. I remember he was in the Slayton hospital for a spell, and then he died.

The pastor said he wouldn't give Uncle Jens a funeral. My grandmother was nearly hysterical because they wouldn't bury her brother. My Dad and grandfather went down to church to argue. After all, Jens was a good man. He took care of his mother himself until she died. He went to church at least on Christmas and Easter. The pastor said that wasn't enough. The argument went on and finally, a service was arranged. However, at the funeral, to everyone's horror, the pastor said Uncle Jens was in hell. My father said he was never going back to church. Later, he would drive his mother but he wouldn't go in.

About this time, my folks wondered what they would do about me and Sunday School. My grandmother had been listening to a radio program from the Sioux City Unitarian Church. Rev. John Brigham, who was the minister, even came to visit my grandparents at Slayton. He talked about how he had worked on a farm in New England. He said that there was a Sunday school program available by mail sent from UUA in Boston.

My dad would have said we were common people. He didn't finish the eighth grade. He had been a hired man and worked on farms. My mother had started college studying music, but got pneumonia and didn't finish. My grandmother, my mother's mother, had to work and hadn't gone to high school. When my mother and grandmother explained Unitarianism, it made sense to my dad right away. He liked that there wasn't a creed. He liked what Rev. Ballou Channing had said that, 'You wouldn't be shut out of the church unless goodness had died in you.' It's hard for me to imagine one of our ministers refusing to provide a funeral for someone because of poor attendance.

We were part of more than one UU congregation by being on the Hanska, Minnesota mailing list as well as the Sioux City, Iowa. The Hanska congregation particularly appealed to my Dad. The Nora Church broke away from Lake Hanska because of fighting over who could be buried in the cemetery. When the Nora church formed one of the first order of business was a new cemetery. Anyone could be buried there no matter what they believed. Even the pastors who refused burial to others were welcomed. My parents and Marilyn are safely there.

What appealed to my father was the church's plainness. You must listen to your conscience and do the right thing. Dad understood the commandments and the Golden Rule. Love of neighbor was a basic value. When a neighbor hurt his arm in a corn picker accident, Dad was off on his Farmall tractor to join our neighbors in bringing in the harvest. Farmers may sound like individualists, but when the chips are down they work together.

Some claim that UU's are hard to understand and read complicated books. How could the average person understand what we believe? Actually, our church requires less philosophy to understand religion. Of course, in other churches, you can simply believe. However, if you start studying the Trinity and the dual nature of Christ, you will find a lot of ancient philosophy that is really very complex. I remember talking to a traditional minister who said he couldn't understand the Christian creed and he had graduated from seminary. You can, of course, turn to philosophy to understand religion and you might enjoy it. It's just that our basics principles aren't all that complicated. They are simple, but not easily lived out.

We appreciate a type of summary called an elevator speech. Can you tell what you believe to a stranger in the time it takes to ride an elevator? This type of summary is an ancient idea going back to the Golden Rule and is found in other religions. One example is "What is hateful to you, do not do to others. This is the whole of Torah. The rest is commentary. Go and study" (Babylonian Talmud, Shabbat 31a). You can say it standing on one foot. The Ames covenant was popular among us: "Love God and love humanity." This affirms what John Dewey suggested in *A Common Faith* that theists and humanists share common ideals.

The UU World editorial that inspired this sermon was skeptical that our traditional value of freedom could have wide appeal. Our oldest American congregations never had creeds. They had covenants. These were agreements about what we were to do, not about what to believe. These covenants go back in some cases to the 1600s. The new behavior covenants that some churches have recently written could be seen are redundant. We always have had agreements about how we were to act. The real problem is honoring them. Because our churches didn't require an exact set of beliefs but a way of behaving, we could embrace a wide number of people who didn't believe exactly the same. Being a farmer, my father never liked being told what to do. The farm itself filled every day with endless demands — it was probably a relief to be able to think for himself.

We have a long history of appealing to the average person. Over a hundred years ago, when Christopher Janson went to the prairie to preach to the Hanska farmers, he found an audience right away. They looked at each other and nudged one another. Afterward, some said they had always thought the way he did, but had been afraid to say so.

Unlike Doug Muder's father, my father always could find someone to talk to in our churches. There is an idea that we are all teachers, scientists, professors, and it is true that some of us are. However, our backgrounds aren't as uniform as some people suppose. Author Herman Melville was also an able seaman, a farmer and a member of All Souls Unitarian Church. One of our great ministers from more than a hundred years ago, Robert Collyer, started as a blacksmith and would use his anvil as a pulpit. Professor James Luther Adams, known for translating theologian Paul Tillich, worked on a farm. He helped his father, who drove a combine pulled by twenty-two horses. To make money for the University of Minnesota, he crawled under trains to fix air brakes. A fellow student with me at our Chicago seminary drove a railroad inspection car. Between churches, another fellow student worked for a milking machine company. A former president of our Chicago seminary worked during WWII setting the triggers in bombs. Another seminary president was once a trucker. When he drove away to a retirement congregation, he rented and packed his own truck to move. Robert Fulgham, whose books were made from his church columns, was once a cowboy as well as an IBM salesman. One of his books, *All I Needed to Know I Learned in Kindergarten,* sold over 15 million books and was translated into 27 languages. We seem to have some common appeal. We have had fishermen, police, truckers, electricians, and firemen in our pulpits and pews.

The editorial author didn't reflect upon the membership of our churches until he had grown up and moved away. As time passed, the membership of our UU churches changed. In New England, the textile mills and shoe factories are gone. Steel plants and other factories closed in the Midwest. One reason that our churches don't have factory workers or other laborers is that these jobs aren't as common as they once were. Manufacturing has declined dramatically, and churches tend to reflect their communities.

Jobs have changed and who we are as a church has changed. I know someone who made feed, but now has a Ph.D. People who once made things are now more likely to provide services. Better paying jobs now require more education. This is true both of farming and manufacturing. Even the military needs people with higher levels of education to maintain and use the equipment. The truth is that we are still mostly made up of working people, but with higher levels of education. Only 10 percent of UU members actually work for themselves. The small drugstores and other stores are now mostly chains and franchises. Even those with good corporate salaries aren't independent. We have a message for working people.

We have congregations with all sorts of people. We have those who based their belief on the biblical heritage and those who just believe in being and doing good. Our message is simple, but that does not mean it is easy. Educator John Dewey in his book *A Common Faith,* thought that people can share common ideals. For example, author Kurt Vonnegut called himself a free thinker and was skeptical of traditional religion. On the other hand, when interviewed on television he would pull out the Golden Rule and the Beatitudes. Like his favorite uncle, he would say, "If that isn't nice, I don't know what is."

Wesley V. Hromatko

We Are Called

In these times, we are called:
Called to step into the mess and murk of life
Called to be strong and vulnerable
Called to console and to challenge
Called to be grounded, and hold lofty ideals
Called to love in the face of hate.

We are called
And it is not easy
And we will not always agree
And we will yell, and scream and cry
And we will laugh and smile and sing.

We are called to be together:
There is so much work to do
And we cannot do it alone
We need one another
Holding each other accountable to our covenants,
to the holy, to love and to do justice.

In these times, we are called.

Darrick Jackson

Fighting the Inner Wounds Of Class Oppression

Every day, envy gnaws at your fingers.
Your eyes watch the movers and shakers
climbing into dream cars, Going Places.
You want to be Somebody. You would ride,
eyes averted from the rear view mirror
where all of the Nobodies recede
like small dark flies to brush away
from smooth white shoulders.

Every day, anger fills your gut like a pile of bricks.
Your own hard shoulders ache to reach in
and hurl them forward one by one.
Your ears would strain to hear the glass
shattering and rubber squealing,
as the fine white shine of the dream machine
careens sidelong off the grade
into a deep obituary.

Every day, you clutch at the bark of trees,
knees trembling, moved and shaken.
Your fingertips feel for hidden messages
left there on some other blue morning when somebody
was repeating poems into gnarled crevices,
quiet voice seeping down the edges of roots
into rock under sand: Remember who you are.
Precious as soil. Worthy of the sun.

Myke Johnson

24

It's Hard Work

The truth is this: If there is no justice, there will be no peace. We can read
Thoreau and Emerson to one another, quote Rilke and Alice Walker and Howard
Thurman, and think good and noble thoughts about ourselves. But if we cannot
bring justice into the small circle of our own individual lives, we cannot hope to
bring justice to the world. And if we do not bring justice to the world, none of us
is safe and none of us will survive. Nothing that Unitarian Universalists need to
do is more important than making justice real – here, where we are. Hard as
diversity is, it is our most important task.
        — *Been in the Storm So Long, by Rosemary Bray McNatt,(1991)*

Ever since reading McNatt's words in seminary, they have sung to me and provided me courage for my work — especially when people have tried to silence me. They have even brought me comfort when I messed up – trying to compare oppressions, denying my own racism or re-centered whiteness.

May McNatt's words bring you courage and comfort in this exciting time of opportunity and healing. May her words bring our entire religion courage and comfort as we narrow the tragic gap between who we are today and who we dream of becoming tomorrow.

May it be so.

Reverend Kellie Kelly

We are Human Beings, Not Human Doings

We are human beings not human doings - there are so many layers to this idea. A large part of my work in Unitarian Universalist at a national level has been around classism: helping our congregations recognize what classism is and recognize how classism plays out in ourselves and in our congregations. And that is hard work. Doing self-examination is just as hard as going out into the community and asking, "What can I do to support you?" Self-examination is not harder nor more important, but it's just as important and just as hard. We need both.

When I first started thinking about the classism I had internalized, I recognized it within my desire to be a UU. I was attracted to the Unitarian Universalist community because I saw you as smart, accomplished and well educated in the formal institutions of our country. At that time, I only had a year and a half of college, so I worked very hard to hide that I wasn't a college graduate. I wouldn't lie, but I wouldn't lead with the fact that I only had a year and a half. I would mention the school that I attended because it's a very prestigious school in the Midwest. I did this name dropping to provide a signal that I belonged to a certain group or class of people, believing that what you do is who you are, where you live is who you are, how much money and assets your family has is who you are. If we take it one step further, not only does this describe who we are, but it determines our worth. So we make these assumptions or connections. We make these connections and we say people who are well educated by our systems of prestige are therefore smarter and more qualified to do many things.

These assumption of worth are extended out in many ways. We know that there is a connection between higher education and what people do for a living, so then we say that people who do certain things are smarter and more qualified. Then we notice that different jobs have different income ranges and can afford people certain assets, so then we start to say that people who are middle class or upper middle class. We may assume that the professional middle class, like ministers and social workers, are smarter and more qualified to do many things. So even if we never say directly anything bad about someone who hasn't gone to college or hasn't finished college or haven't said anything

directly bad about people who are struggling financially, we can't have one without the other. We can't assume that one group is more qualified, more more deserving or more intelligent if there is not another group to compare them too. That inferior group is filled with people who were not able to get that education, their brains just don't get excited by academia or they enjoy employing skills other than the Socratic method (which if faced with a pop quiz, I couldn't tell you exactly what the Socratic method is, but if I could, I would be tempted to see this knowledge as putting me into a loftier group of people). But people, we are not human doings, we are human beings.

When I became a separated single mom soon to become a divorced single mom, I didn't want my son's quality of life to change. I felt embarrassed about what I was going to do financially. That went away when I started seminary, because I was able to say, "Oh, I am not poor because I am a single mom, I am poor because I am a grad student. Eventually, I am going to study to become a minister and I am going to be part of the system. This means I am actually better and more deserving, than if I was working as a secretary or a sales person, struggling to make ends meet for my child and myself." It took me a long time to realize how much I had internalized the classism that our culture teachers us. Lessons on classism are embedded in our culture — it is in the water, in the air and often it works with racism.

Classism shows up in racism by making us think that only certain things belong with certain races. Quite often classism has been used as a tool to increase the racism of poor white people. Our media sends the message that everyone worthy in the United States is middle class — working class white people or struggling lower middle class people. Consequently, no one wants to admit that they are poor and no one wants to admit that they are rich, because both of those things can mean that there is something wrong with you. You are either very greedy or you made a lot of poor choices. As Unitarian Universalists, we know we all are part of these class systems, and that the critical choice we face is to let these systems go unquestioned or work against these systems of classism.

But my question for our Beloved UU community is: how do we find a way to stop being part of that doing culture which values people for what they do more than for who they are, while we still value doing the work of justice? So many people cannot do the work of getting a petition to the state house or the white house because they are working 14 hours a day to support their own house — they don't have paid time off or even the flexibility of taking a day off without the assurance that they won't have a job tomorrow. But aren't these people valued members of our Beloved community? So how do we balance this need to see ourselves as more than what we do, yet still make sure that we are working hard to dismantle these systems that tell us that one person is worth more than another person because of their education, the neighborhood they live in, or the color of their skin?

I've was torn inside during this time of the pandemic. I know many of us were bored out of our minds — but wasn't that boredom in and of itself a luxury? I have seen poems and prayers inviting us to look upon this time as a sabbath of rest. I know that there is beauty and wisdom in that perspective, but I know for so many people within our country, this has not been a true sabbath. It was the only a day, a week, a month or several months in which they didn't get paid and they fell further and further behind those with privilege.

One of our congregants sent me a poem that has gone viral. I don't know if they sent it to me because they saw the title of our service for today or if it was a happy coincidence. It is a poem by Kitty O'Meara. O'Meara is a retired Irish American teacher and I think that her words strike an important balance between using this time to pause to contemplate who we think we are, and taking this time to hear that part of our brain we try not to pay attention to — the worry, anxiety and despair around us. Yes, we can use our boredom to give ourselves some time for rest and reflection, or we can allow ourselves to grieve the huge loss of freedom, our sense of community and the people of our neighborhoods.

To think that we are all going to remain untouched by this pandemic is just impossible. Over 600,000 people died in New York yesterday. In one day. Yes, there are disasters like hurricanes, earthquakes and tornadoes, and this pandemic has been just as devastating. We can talk about how our country administration's and the world's governments have failed us, yet no matter how hard hard we work to change our imperfect systems, bad things will happen to good people and death comes for all of us.

It makes sense that we would want to stay busy and not think about that; how could we go out into the world if we thought every time we left our loved ones we may never see them again? Yet this is a time where we can try to extend ourselves and see how much we can balance simply being with still doing. We can know and hold our fears and anxieties, and know that if we hold them for just a little while, they will not swallow us whole. We will be able to come back to each other, and ourselves stronger. We are not just our occupations, we are not just what we do, we can be silent and listen and still do the work of justice.

O'Meara's Words: And the People Stayed Home

And the people stayed home
And read books and listened and rested and exercised
and made art and played games and learned new ways of being
and were still
and listened more deeply.

Some meditated, some prayed, some danced
Some met their shadows and
the people began to think differently
and the people healed,
and in the absence of people living in
ignorant, dangerous mindless and heartless ways,
the earth began to heal
and when the danger passed and the people joined together again
they grieved their losses and made new choices
and dreamed new images and created new ways to live
and heal the earth as fully as they had been healed.

O'Meara's words remind us that we don't have to choose between being and doing. As we value who we are as beings, we are healed and we bring healing to the earth. When we get caught up in valuing ourselves by what we do, we will come to point when we cannot do any more, and think that our worth is in question. But our value does not diminish with our age or our health. Our first UU principle about "The inherent worth and dignity of every human being" extends to everyone — a two month old baby or a ninety-eight year old elder, people struggling with classism, people oppressed by racism — we are all worthwhile. This isn't about isms —classism or racism — these are very real problems and we need to be working on them, but we also need to work on seeing each other as valuable human beings. We are so much more than what we say and do, and if we can give ourselves time to value and appreciate our humanity, then maybe healing will come to us both individually and collectively.

Reverend Kelli Kelly

Class Stories: Embracing Our Diversity

I am going to start this conversation with two short readings. The first one is from a book called Class Lives: Stories from Across our Economic Divide by Chuck Collins, Jennifer Ladd, Maynard Seider, and Felice Yeskel.

> "Sometimes I think of class as our collective national family secret. And as any therapist will tell you, family secrets are problematic. Most of us believe that the United States is a classless society, one that is basically middle class, except for a few unfortunate poor people and some lucky rich ones. We have been taught from childhood myths and misconceptions around class, mobility and the American dream. Many of us are confused about class and don't tend to think about it consciously, as we might our race, ethnicity, gender, religion, age, or sexual orientation. Nonetheless, our class identity has a huge impact on every aspect of our lives — from parenting style to the way we speak, from what we dare to dream to the likelihood we will spend time in prison, from how we spend our days to how many days we have."

My second reading is from Doug Muder, who is a journalist and editor for our magazine UU World. He wrote an article on the principles in 2014 which stated:

> "The point of putting the principles in the front of the hymnal and teaching them to our children isn't to assert their truth or even to encourage you to nod along with the idea that they should be true. Unitarian Universalism is a commitment to envision a world in which the principles have become true, to envision it so intensely and in such detail that it becomes a genuine possibility and to join with others in making these possibilities real."

Class tends to not be a popular conversation piece for most conversations, so I'm going to try to make this as painless as possible. I have been involved with an organization called UU Class Conversations since my first year in seminary, and for me they provided a bridge so that I could stay in seminary and, to be frank, so that I could stay in the Unitarian Universalist faith.

My background looks very much like what we tend to think of as the stereotype for Unitarian Universalists. I'm good at typing in the right time and not sharing information that might show me as an outsider. Well, I used to be good at it. Now I tell my story a little bit more often. And so when I came to Unitarian Universalism, I was excited to see a faith that was so welcoming.

One of the congregations that I spent time at was the Unitarian Church of Norfolk, Virginia. Their welcome is still one of my favorites, and I'd like to share it with you: "Whatever your faith, whatever the country of your heritage, you are welcome here. Whoever you are, whomever you love, you are welcome here. And whether you entered on little feet or walked in briskly or ambled or rolled in, you are welcome here. We are glad that you chose our congregation as your place of worship today."

That welcome embodies our principles, especially our first principle, the inherent worth and dignity of every person. This principle attracted me to Unitarian Universalism. However, I somewhat naively thought that if I pointed out that sometimes Unitarian Universalism is a little bit exclusionary to people who don't have a master's degree or a doctorate, that everyone would be really excited and say, "Thank you for pointing that out! We didn't realize that. Let's make some changes." But the reality is that the reaction I get is more like in the story of *The Emperor's New Clothes,* and it doesn't go very well.

When everyone sees the Emperor go through the city in his new clothes, which consists of no clothing at all, a child yells out that he's not wearing any clothes. I somehow thought that the Emperor put on a robe and invited the child back for tea to celebrate his honesty. That's not quite how it happens. So when I started talking about class, I found both at my seminary and at the churches that I was in that people didn't want to talk about it. They told me that this is just how it is.

But what I've seen as I've worked with you through UU's Class Conversations that there are people who want to talk about where they fit in to our culture and they want to be part of the solution. So it's easy to complain within an organization and say "they're doing this or they're doing that." And to be frank, there are several Facebook groups where Unitarian Universalists from blue collar backgrounds talk and complain about other Unitarian Universalists, forgetting that they are also Unitarian Universalists. We are all Unitarian Universalists, and if we want to make our faith community, both on a local level and also on a national level, more welcoming and inclusive, then it's our responsibility to stop othering, stop complaining and make it so. What UU Class Conversations does is it goes to congregations and gets these hard conversations started.

What I have found by being a facilitator is that healing is able to start. People come up to me with tears in their eyes and talk about how they came from a background where their parents didn't graduate from high school, and because of the different programs and incentives, they were able to not only finish high school and their bachelor's degree, but they were also able to become a University Professor. However, this is the secret that they've been holding not really feeling comfortable talking about it and sharing their full selves with their beloved congregations. Some of these members at various churches have been members for 30 or 40 years, keeping this part of themselves separate. So what I would like to encourage us to do is to start sharing more of our stories, whether that's a class story, a story about our background in a different country, a story about our background in a different religion.

We have so much to share with each other and yet if we hide who we are, we can't fully be here in an authentic way. So one of the things that I learned was that every class group has both strengths and limitations.

Reverend Kellie Kelly

Breaking the Chains of Poverty

Leader: Spirit of Love, Life and Justice,

All: **Hear the cries of your people!**

Leader: For all who are trapped in poverty;

All: **Bring your freedom and fullness of life.**

Leader: For all who struggle with insufficient income;

All: **Bring employment and creative new ways of earning a living.**

Leader: For all who are weighed down by mounting debt;

All: **Bring release and an end to this burden.**

Leader: For all who lay blame on those who suffer;

All: **Open their eyes to the oppressive systems at play.**

Leader: For all who seek a more equitable future;

All: **Bring a hunger for change that fuels real solutions.**
                     Amen.

Kate Lore

Prayer for Economic Hardship

Great Mystery at the Heart of All Life,

In this time of economic insecurity, I call out to you! I know that your love is infinite and that you care about all areas of my life. Draw near to me now that I might feel your presence.

Today I am drowning in debt and despair. Help me calm these storms raging within and around me. Release this tension in my body. Tame my worries and calm my heart that I might sleep.

Guide me out of this hardship and mess. Infuse me with your creativity and keep my creditors at bay until I can find new solutions. Help me trust that I am enough, the world is enough, and all will be well.

Merciful One, you are my lifeline. Apart from you I am lost, hopeless and doomed. With you, I keep my head above water until my feet find land once more. With a humble heart, I say: "Thank you and Amen."

Kate Lore

Oh, you don't need to have a Ph.D.
To make conversation with folks like me,
For we're UU, the same as you,
And that's how it ought to be.
First time I visited things went sour
When I showed up at the coffee hour,
Folks only asked where I went to college;
Seemed like they were testing my knowledge.
Now some UUs eat black-eyed peas;
Some drink fine wine with fancy cheese.
Some of our families are doing real well;
Some have been struggling for quite a spell.
Some of our children are quite successful,
Others have issues and lives that are stressful.
Some go to public, some to private, schools,
Some learn at home, with different rules.
Real UUs don't need to be clannish
Though some speak Arabic and some speak Spanish,
Some have an accent or a Southern drawl,
But we're real UUs, the same as y'all.

Betty Jo Middleton

U. U. Blue Collar Blues

Words by Betty Jo Middleton

Music by Liam Battjes-Greenwood

Oh, you don't_ need to have a P. H. D._____ to make con-ver-sa-tion with some folks like me___'coz we're U. U. the same as you__ and that's how

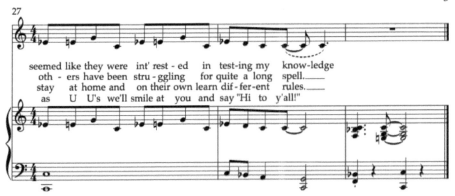

seemed like they were int' rest - ed   in   test-ing my   know-ledge
oth - ers have been stru - ggling   for quite a long   spell.___
stay   at home and   on their own learn dif - fer-ent   rules.___
as   U   U's we'll smile at   you and say "Hi to   y'all!"

Pandemic Benediction

Look at your hands. If you are with another person you can safely touch, maybe you could hold hands.

These are the hands that do the work of the world. The hands of those who tend to us in the hospital, who deliver our mail, who grow our food, who ring up our groceries, who struggle with Zoom to teach our children. These are the hands that play music and the hands that applaud them, the hands that garden, make bread, and sew masks. These are the hands that carry protest signs and write letters to voters they will never meet.

May they be blessed in their work.

Amen.

Reverend Millie Phillips

Today, Notice the Class Diversity Around You – and Listen

When you walk into a room full of people, I bet you unconsciously notice the race and gender make up of the group (or what you assume people's races and genders are; sometimes we all guess wrong); it doesn't take conscious thought to be aware that you have similar or different identities than most of the others. The same is not true of social class. Often we don't know the class background or even the current class of those we encounter, as many class indicators are invisible to the eye, or ambiguous.

Approximately 2/3 of US adults don't have a college degree; most Americans are employed in closely supervised jobs with less autonomy, less authority and less respect given to their expertise than professionals or managers have. That is, most Americans are working class. About 1/3 of Americans are renters. More than one in 10 are living below the poverty line at any given time.

Working-class and poverty-class Americans are disproportionately people of color, but the majority are white; they are disproportionately elderly and children, but include all ages; they are disproportionately women, but include all genders; they are disproportionately new refugees and undocumented immigrants, but the majority are citizens. All of us, regardless of our own class, live surrounded by diverse working-class and poor people—but most of us never stop to notice the class make-up of a situation, or the class inequities around us.

But we should notice.To live up to the first UU Principle of upholding the worth and dignity of every human being we need to deliberately give our attention and respect to people of all classes. And to live up to the second UU Principle of justice, equity and compassion in human relations we need to challenge the class inequities affecting the working-class and poverty-class people who are part of us. But our unjust society makes this work difficult to do.

Today, you can start by asking yourself, 'Whose voices am I listening to?' Run through your typical day. Maybe you wake up and turn on the radio, or open the newspaper or the online news site; the journalists whose words inform you are virtually all college-educated and professional-middle-class. When they talk about the economy, do they interview anyone coping with its downside? Do you subscribe to anything containing content created by working-class or poverty-class people?

Today, the odds are that someone will be serving you, whether at a coffeeshop, a salon or barbershop or a gas pump. Will you tune in to them as particular people with other interests than just serving you? Whose names do you know? Whose back stories have you heard? Are there small ways you can make things better for them? Tipping well is obvious, and giving 5-star reviews; but sometimes you can also adjust your behavior to inconvenience them less, speak up if you see them mistreated, or affirm what they do.

If your workplace or school is a big institution, you probably hear often from the senior management about how the organization is doing. How often do you hear the perspectives of the support staff? How much time do you spend talking with those in working-class jobs in different parts of the organization than your own? Those closest to a problem often have the best understanding of its causes. What solutions might be overlooked by not drawing out the views of those working on the physical plant, food, direct-care human services, administrative support and so on?

When you give away money, whether small or big amounts, how often do you give to nonprofits run by working-class or poor people — where the people directly affected by the social problem have a say in what the organization does? Do you judge a charity by the persuasive words of its professional staff, or do you meet the people served or organized? Before donating, do you find out how much a nonprofit's support staff earns or whether they get health benefits?

Your elected officials are probably all highly educated homeowners, living in the more expensive part of the district. How in touch are they with working-class and poor constituents? Do you base your vote on that question? In your town, when decisions are made about affordable housing and zoning, are the decision-makers all homeowners, as is true in most towns? Shouldn't people in need of affordable housing be represented?

And what about your UU church? Your congregation is probably more diverse in class background than you realize, and maybe in current class, too. But are the working-class and poverty-class members known to each other and to other congregants? Are you one of them? Do you know if any congregants experience any church practices as classist, demeaning or exclusionary to members like themselves? Does your diversity, equity and inclusion work include class, not just underrepresented racial and gender identities? Thanks to UU Class Conversations, a few congregations do have working-class identity groups, class-conscious social justice programming, and/or classism workshops—but most do not.

Whatever your own class, whether or not you are working-class yourself, whether or not you have working-class family members, it requires being proactive to hear working-class and poverty-class voices as loudly as the professional-middle-class (PMC) voices that ring most loudly throughout our society. What can you do, in your specific settings and spheres of influence, to listen with a better class balance?

Perhaps this sounds like a guilt trip, or a dutiful thing you should do. But actually, diversifying your life more by class can be full of satisfactions. Several times I have gone through this kind of transition: living in an upper-middle-class neighborhood and then moving into a working-class or high-poverty neighborhood; working an office job with other professionals and then switching to a grassroots community organizing job — and let me tell you, it's like that moment in the *Wizard of Oz* when the movie goes from black-and-white to technicolor.

Why? College-educated people of all races and genders have been taught to talk in certain ways and to adhere to the norms of a professional workplace. There's often one 'right' way to respond to a situation. Speaking as a college-educated professional myself, I recognize this homogeneity in myself and my class-peers, including those with warm hearts and progressive values, but those are expressed in a fairly uniform way. Research shows that those of us who get professional-middle-class socialization make our speech more abstract; we restrain our emotional expression; we alter our behavior at work to fit in with the culture of mostly white male senior managers, and, to varying degrees, that affects our communication style at home too. At UUCC workshops, some participants have complained about a low-key style and subdued emotional tone within UU congregations, and I recognize that as a PMC class-cultural style.

Working-class and poverty-class Americans, by contrast, are marvelously multicultural, more likely to be rooted in their ethnic traditions. They are more likely to stay in their hometowns as adults and so are more immersed in local culture, for example keeping their accents and local lingo, and knowing where the best pizza, beer or ethnic food can be found. Humor styles are more varied, and usually humor plays a bigger role in conversations. In some working-class cultures, it's fine to be dramatic and emotional in ways that are defined as 'inappropriate' in some professional-middle-class spaces.

So diversify your social life for yourself too! Vary the voices you listen to, reach out to connect to more class-disadvantaged people in your life and in the wider world. Expand your world, yes, out of solidarity; Yes, as part of your commitment to UU principles; Yes, to seek better solutions for social problems; Yes, because it may make a difference to others —but also do it for yourself! Your world could be fuller and brighter than it is now.

Betsy Leondar-Wright

Author Biographies

Elizabeth Cogliati

Elizabeth is Director of Lifespan Faith Development at the Unitarian Universalist Church in Idaho Falls, Idaho. She is also the social justice chair for the congregation. While previously working for the Office of Rural Health in Bozeman, Montana, she helped write and execute a survey of all the churches and social welfare organizations in Montana.

Barbara Cogswell

Barbara was born in Kansas City, Kansas in January 1933, just 3 years before the Ford Motor Co strike which left her dad out of work. He did odd jobs wherever he found them, to keep food on the table, until he got back pay and we moved to a 20-acre piece of land with a creek on it. Her dad built a temporary house from pieces of boxes in which coffins were transported. This made for a very spartan shelter. He dug a well, bought a cow, and put in a large garden, tomatoes potatoes, green beans, onions and strawberries, which my Mother canned and preserved. He began to quarry rock for the foundation of a house which was left unfinished until WW II ended and Barbara was in the 8th Grade.

Chuck Collins

Chuck is an author and a senior scholar at the Institute for Policy Studies in Washington, DC, where he directs the Program on Inequality and the Common Good. He is also co-founder of Wealth for Common Good. He is an expert on economic inequality in the US, and has pioneered efforts to bring together investors and business leaders to speak out publicly against corporate practices and economic policies that increase economic inequality.

Jason Cook

Reverend Jason Cook currently serves the Unitarian Universalist Congregation in Fullerton, California. He has also served as the Admissions Director for Meadville Lombard Theological School. Jason's extended family members are mostly located in rural Indiana, the state he was born and raised in. He lives with his husband in the diverse community of Santa Ana and can be found many evenings on the local stage performing in a variety of plays.

Thomas Earthman

Thomas is the founder and administrator for the I Am UU project. He is passionate about building a better world and a beloved community, and he feels that liberal religion is a vital tool in that construction, and that Unitarian Universalism is the best vehicle for introducing liberal religion to the majority of North America.

Mike Greenwood

Mike's first UU Class Conversations workshop was in 2015. He has been an ardent supporter ever since. A native Vermonter, Mike spent most of his life in southern New England where he was a teacher and staff developer for the Windsor Public Schools as well as with the Connecticut State Department of Education. After 35 years in education, Mike retired and returned home to Vermont. He resides in Vergennes with his husband Liam and their adopted dog, Flapjack.

Wesley V. Hromatko

Wesley Hromatko currently is a speaker and provides pulpit supply in the Minnesota, Iowa and South Dakota Tri-State area. He lives at and operates Minnesota Century Farm. He has also written biographical articles for the UUHS as well as other articles including those in the New Encyclopedia of Unbelief. In addition to serving Unitarian Universalist congregations, he has also participated in denominational organizations such as the Chicago Area UU Conference. His education started in a one room school before graduating from the University of Minnesota and ended at the University of Chicago and Meadville/Lombard Theological School in Chicago which awarded him the doctor of ministry, D.Min.

Darrick Jackson

The Reverend Darrick Jackson (he/him) is the Director of Ministries for Lifelong Learning of UU Ministers Association and an Affiliated Community Minister with Second Unitarian Church of Chicago. He is one of the authors in the book "Centering: Navigating Race, Authenticity and Power in Ministry." Reverend Darrick is active in DRUUMM (the UU ministry for people of color, and is the treasurer for Healing Moments (a ministry for caregivers of people with Alzheimer's). He is also Co-Associate Director of the Chicago Playback Theatre Ensemble and is an avid knitter. Rev. Darrick and his husband, Reverend James Olson, live with their two cats, Merlin and Morgana.

Myke Johnson

Myke Johnson is the author of Finding Our Way Home: A Spiritual Journey into Earth Community, and also blogs at a site of the same name. She grew up white and working class, mostly in Michigan. Going to college and then encountering the Catholic Worker movement opened up new possibilities in her life. She became a peace and justice activist, feminist, witch, lesbian, anti-racist, writer, and eventually was ordained a UU minister in 1999. Ministry brought her to Portland, Maine to serve the Allen Avenue UU Church in 2005. She retired because of chronic illness in 2018. She lives with her partner Margy Dowzer, cats Billie and Sassy, and many birds, squirrels, frogs, trees and other beings who share the backyard where she is learning to garden.

Kellie Kelly

Kellie identifies as a white person who was raised in poverty by a single mom and from generations of poverty. She spent many volunteer hours with Jobs for Justice, and has served as a community organizer and as the Social Justice Minister First of Unitarian of Portland, Oregon. When she informed her husband that she wanted a divorce, he locked her and the kids out of the house and emptied out the savings. They were left homeless and penniless. Her writings and work come out of knowing pain and worry, and now this fuels her work in helping others facing economic hardship and uncertainly.

Kate Lore

A graduate of Meadville/Lombard School of Theology, Kate Lore is currently the senior minister at Quimper Unitarian Universalist Fellowship in Port Townsend, Washington. Prior to that time, she served as the Social Justice Minister at First Unitarian Church of Portland, Oregon. In her free time, Kate enjoys kayaking, hiking and thinking big. Her latest project involves developing a "cottage community" on the land abutting QUUF to increase Port Townsend's stock of affordable housing units.

Betty Jo Middleton

Reverend Betty Jo Middleton is retired from the Unitarian Universalist Ministry of Religious Education. She served eight congregations and was on the field staff of the Unitarian Universalist Association. She is the author of *To Touch Inward Springs: Teaching and Learning for Faith Development* and religious education materials for all ages. Betty Jo has taught courses in two theological schools. She lives in Alexandria, Virginia, where she spends much of her time writing poetry.

Millie Phillips

Reverend Millie Phillips' class background is ambivalent. Her housewife mother grew up in poverty; her high school teacher father in a middle-class environment. Her parents were downwardly mobile due to ongoing medical crises and she spent a decade of being very low-income as a young adult. After learning a blue-collar trade, she gained relative affluence and spent many years as a grateful union activist. Retiring in her 50s, she studied for the ministry and was ordained right before the pandemic. Laid off from her one ministry position, she now works in Concord CA as a "faith-rooted organizer" for the Faith Alliance for a Moral Economy.

Betsy Leondar-Wright

Betsy Leondar-Wright, PhD, was a founding member of UU Class Conversations and is a long-time board member of Class Action, www.classism.org. Her book, *Missing Class: Strengthening Social Movement Groups by Seeing Class Cultures* (Cornell University Press, 2014) grew out of her research on 25 diverse social justice groups. She is an associate professor of sociology at Lasell University. A long-time activist for economic justice, she was the Communications Director for nine years at United for a Fair Economy, where she co-authored *The Color of Wealth: The Story Behind the US Racial Wealth Divide* (2006). Since writing *Class Matters: Cross-Class Alliance Building for Middle-Class Activists* (2005), Betsy has led over 200 workshops all over the US on classism, cross-class alliance building, class cultures, the racial wealth divide, and economic inequality. She grew up in an upper-middle-class family in a mixed-class New Jersey suburb.

Appendix

Chalice Lightings, Readings and Sermon Prompts

Chuck Collins writes, "I realize that I never write out a sermon, since I don't read them. So I have a series of prompts, story prompts etc."

Waking Up White – *Debby Irving*

My glorification of independence and individualism made me an easy target for the myth of meritocracy and overshadowed in my heart what I knew to be true; the deep interconnectedness I longed for with family, friends, colleagues, and even strangers is core to human survival. Interdependence is our lifeblood.

Inequality Matters – *Jared Bernstein*

Inequality directly undermines equality of opportunity, likely through a variety of mechanisms. As the gap between the rich and poor widens, lower-income families have less ability relative to their rich counterparts to invest in enrichment goods for their children. Children from families with less income have relatively less extensive and privileged social networks and, compared to their rich peers, are more likely to experience the type of "toxic" stress that can hamper brain development and long-term academic, health, and economic outcomes.

Inequality is the Root of Social Evil – *Pope Francis*

As long as the problems of the poor are not radically resolved by rejecting the absolute autonomy of markets and financial speculation and by attacking the structural causes of inequality, no solution will be found for the world's problems or, for that matter, to any problems. Inequality is the root of social ills. As long as the problems of the poor are not radically resolved by rejecting the absolute autonomy of markets and financial speculation and by attacking the structural causes of inequality, no solution will be found for the world's problems or, for that matter, to any problems. Inequality is the root of social ills.

Living Between Two Stories – *Charles Eisenstein*

The world as we know it is built on a story. To be a change agent is, first, to disrupt the existing Story of the World, and second, to tell a new Story of the World so that those entering the space between stories have a place to go. Often, these two functions merge into one, since the actions we take that are part of the telling of a new story are also disruptive to the old. We do not have a new story yet. Each of us is aware of some of its threads, for example in most of the things we call alternative, holistic, or ecological today. Here and there we see patterns, designs, emerging parts of the fabric. But the new mythos has not yet emerged. We will abide for a time in the space between stories. Those of you who have been through it on a personal level know that it is a very precious – some might say sacred – time. Then we are in touch with the real. Each disaster lays bare the real underneath our stories. The terror of a child, the grief of a mother, the honesty of not knowing why. In such moments we discover our humanity. We come to each other's aid, human to human. We take care of each other. That's what keeps happening every time there is a calamity, before the beliefs, the ideologies, the politics take over again. Events like Sandy Hook, for at least a moment, cut through all that down to the basic human being. In such times, we learn who we really are.

A Paradise Built in Hell: The Extraordinary Communities That Arise in Disaster –
Rebecca Solnit

When I studied disasters past, what amazed me was not just that people behaved so beautifully, but that, in doing so, they found such joy. It seems that something in their natures, starved in ordinary times, was fed by the opportunity, under the worst of conditions, to be generous, brave, Quote--idealistic, and connected; and when this appetite was fulfilled, the joy shone out, even amid the ruins.

From Charles Eisenstein...

The breakdown of the old story is kind of a healing process, that uncovers the old wounds hidden under its fabric and exposes them to the healing light of awareness. I am sure many people reading this have gone through such a time, when the cloaking illusions fell away: all the old justifications, rationalizations, all the old stories. Events like Sandy Hook help to initiate the very same process on a collective level. So also the superstorms, the economic crisis, political meltdowns... in one way or another, the obsolescence of our old mythos is laid bare.

We do not have a new story yet. Each of us is aware of some of its threads, for example in most of the things we call alternative, holistic, or ecological today. Here and there we see patterns, designs, emerging parts of the fabric. But the new mythos has not yet emerged. We will abide for a time in the space between stories. Those of you who have been through it on a personal level know that it is a very precious – some might say sacred – time. Then we are in touch with the real. Each disaster lays bare the real underneath our stories. The terror of a child, the grief of a mother, the honesty of not knowing why. In such moments we discover our humanity. We come to each other's aid, human to human. We take care of each other. That's what keeps happening every time there is a calamity, before the beliefs, the ideologies, the politics take over again. Events like Sandy Hook, for at least a moment, cut through all that down to the basic human being. In such times, we learn who we really are.

Quotes

Arundhati Roy:

> Another world is not only possible, she is on her way. On a quiet day, I can hear her breathing.

Eve Ensler:

> The tyranny of masculinity and the tyranny of patriarchy…has been much more deadly to men than it has to women. It hasn't killed our hearts. It's killed men's hearts. It's silenced them; it's cut them off.

Gloria Steinem:

> We'll never solve the feminization of power until we solve the masculinity of wealth.

James Baldwin:

> Any real change implies the breakup of the world as one has always known it, the loss of all that gave one an identity, the end of safety. And at such a moment, unable to see and not daring to imagine what the future will now bring forth, one clings to what one knew, or dreamed that one possessed. Yet, it is only when a man is able, without bitterness or self-pity, to surrender a dream he has long cherished or a privilege he has long possessed that he is set free — he has set himself free — for higher dreams, for greater privileges.